"The poems in _____ _____ ____ ind wonderfully sm _____ _____ ge, she unearths new ___ ___ ___ ___ and struggling to say. Her work, rooted in the tongue, shows how speaking becomes a physical affirmation of a self. Led by the music of the monosyllable, use of sound is sometimes breathless, sometimes fractured, but always new. These are poems that beat forth urgently, and I listen, wholly rapt, as she interrogates the effects of violence on black girls, what it means to be a black woman, and how one is strengthened by giving voice to brokenness."

—Jennifer K. Sweeney, author of *Little Spells,*
How to Live on Bread and Music, Salt Memory

"In the astonishing *us mouth*, we encounter a space of rigorous linguistic constraint and radical poetic abandon. Chaney's poems deftly occupy the tension between these two poles. Through her controlled, ecstatic technique, she excavates and fractures categories of race, gender, family, the body, bureaucracy, semantics, and history, re-igniting and re-investing them with real complexity and deep beauty. Nikia Chaney is a dazzling, daring poet; her book is an exhilarating experience that reminds us what poetic experiments can do."

—Alistair McCartney, author of *The Disintegrations*

"I wish I could apprentice my craft and my very body to these embodied poems that traffic in language and power, using a pattern of everything unexpected, and moving along a strand of pull, rise, and drop. Perilous, outrageous, Chaney's lines sport hairpin turns, syntax that lingoes and sputters, short lines that aphorize and fragment, then longer ones and invented forms opening at last into newness, possibility. To me, these poems are as smart in form as they are in concept: world change, world stubborn, world wise. They raise into a reader's imagination a place where sex with a man can mean both love and violence, where family history, once restored, stabilizes but doesn't stable, where the mother must rise into her own skin to hold the baby who is half child and half herself. And they gesture always, even at their most personal, to the possibility that there is an "us." Nikia Chaney has always been one to watch. Now she's one to follow!"

—Jenny Factor, author of *Unraveling at the Name*

us mouth is irreducible. *us mouth* is "maw" ("tongue that /cracks / thunder..."). *us mouth* regenerates genre. *us mouth* knows odds and hopes are choices, as Chaney's inimitable lyricism and astonishing voices leap quick bops, strum long aubades, and unfold odes. *us mouth* is "the next / now." *us mouth* is girls tweaking in units; "Mermaids twerking on candied feet;" a life in bullet pointed "collateral contacts;" a mother singing her little boy and the little boy within his great grandfather in "Tennesee where /boys limbs and skin fed /sugar cane or else the unyielding / ideas of property." *us mouth* releases seeds yielding fields of meaning; *us mouth* takes root in sidewalk and in sky; *us mouth* eats the bird crushed underfoot and is eaten by the hummingbird in flight. *us mouth* is all and one, after and before. And above all, Chaney's poetry opens the heart so that, like the hummingbird's "numbing / made of many /wings" our heart yields. Takes it all in. Murmurs for more."

—Julie Sophia Paegle, author of *Twelve Clocks*

us mouth

live learn teach do!

us mouth

HELL PRESS
UNIVERSITY OF HELL PRESS

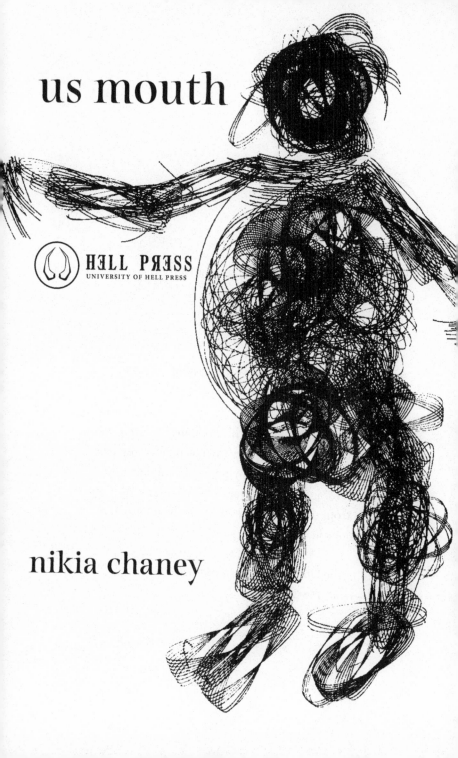

nikia chaney

HELL PRESS
UNIVERSITY OF HELL PRESS

This book is published by University of Hell Press
www.universityofhellpress.com

© 2018 Nikia Chaney

Cover and Interior Design by Olivia Croom
http://bit.ly/oliviacroom

Published in the United States of America
ISBN 978-1-938753-27-5

Contents

A book is never one's own. It is simply a collection of voices nurtured by the inhabitants of the spaces all around. And all my spaces have been filled with such beautiful souls. We breathe, we sing, we eat, we kiss, we mouth, together.

Thank you California State University, San Bernardino, San Bernardino Valley College, Antioch University, Cave Canem, San Bernardino Generation Now, the Garcia Center for the Arts, and the Inlandia Institute. Thank you so much editors and staff of University of Hell Press for working with me and bringing this book to life. I can only hope one day to repay all you have done for me.

And thank you bubba, shushu, billa, yusuf, and riya, for always giving mama 15 more minutes to write.

So much love!

why you acting like

it ain't right the reap the take
the ritual
of flirting like we warm pickings only just to
be inserted
in and it doesn't have a billion harvests every
penny we spend spins beneath a
bridge or hatchery
of collected parts of the forest groaning bold
in our wake
while wax pushes out with
this middling between our pelvic your mouth
sucking on our skin and this
sucking this
plunge for oxygen and recognition
is more so sin than
survival toss your skin to the chapter
of our lust no slice gleam here just
your nags sifting out my fingers
your hatchet
sweaty like you burning
baby your girl
so much better than a minstrel the men riding
bikes the women frying
heads running fool for a circus show bowing
you think your leech of me
can clear us both
adapt to this man I have to say it and drag
you out spit on your black blues
burst your beauty open like a fissure where

your freak bush is agnostic hopeful and alert and I
wail your name
on purpose

kept

I think   across some raised surface.
I am   at least gold.
                prone.
  alive
kneeling   leased   burnt night   bump of touch treat.
   think I am   prowling again some idle
         whole.   heat filled knife.   quiet that flits.
                                                        around me.
                  if there was   street.
only   a small spring spilling in
     my back   the bones of my neck   a way to lose.
   an earring.   break the glass   fins even
                                                make loose.
I would not
         keep   bubbles of need.
circling   pipes
circling high
     this wet thing.

the shakes

I shakes ease eat re
dead nails click kinged tales.
    I taste trees code every
    key that cakes the tickle

dead. Nails clicking details.
I arm out banshee bone
    key. At cay keys that tickle
code by ways. And

    I arm mount. Band. She bone
    peas take locks that
coal gyrate. She and
        worst. A hand hurt sense

    pea stake locks that
I taste. I crack we's
        Worse. I tower and hurt. Sins
that feed. The share sold bait.

        I taste I. Crack we is
need whole been grapes
        the feed the shares. Old bait
in the pens. Dance pop vein

need whole. Been gray. Pass
    peace take locks that
in deep. Ends. Ants pop vain
        plot ice click and wing.

Please. Stake glocks in that.
I tastier. Scold every
pot I lick I sang. Sing.
I shakes these eaters. See.

every tree

my father
must have been
a boy I
talked to his
mother once when he
died I was nine
teen and on the phone her
voice dripped down
acidic and plump and
sweet as
if she really knew
me as his
child I saw
her stooped soft with
plate whine
touch and I
questioned what she said
she saw of her
boy in the picture
I had sent his nose his
coloring the nightmare he
had at three where his baby
shrill screaming had not yet
turned to rumbling
speak of his
pride last night
in the dark of early
morning I felt like clapping
when we hung up

the phone my
mother's father
must have been
a black boy a black
little boy this would
have been Tennessee where
boys limbs and skin fed
sugar cane or else the unyielding
ideas of property my mother
telling me that this
boy her father was not
one to work
hard one of those
men who danced
and drank down women with
his teeth and he gave
my sister his green
eyes in another
stratifying scheme I don't know
the name of trees all
this forest
around me the exact
same sapling and
applaud and
ripped palms and
hardness of palm and
hairiness then
shocking smoothness of back these
men these yet I still find
the best way to describe
things here the
makeup of sugar

pine the way aspen habits
its way into growth or the reason
why I cannot roll
my tongue answered sorted
information to search
for to find like a phone
call to a woman
I don't know I
wish I
could have been
a black boy growing
up by some
unspoken agreement I
had to be
the ken doll when
we played the plastic's
hardness his blond
fro more familiar to
me than my
own soft face my
own ability
to hide was
this the lesson that
men learned as
boys black boys the
combination and
clarity transforming limbs to
bark to screams and
when I learned that
black boys are unknowable
unknowing or un
knead I changed

my mind I hold here on
my lap this
little black boy who
came out of my own
body I
put his arm in
the forest dirt wash his
back his teeth and feet clap
chin palm to earth
to palm with needle
like leaves name him scream
his name in the dim
green silence again again
again so
that he might
speak and turn to
me and not
ask me mama who who
when

tell me grinning man

what is home

    but a prone brother's body
stiff with the promise
        of fiction of sweat of no woman left behind of eat of this flesh

    tell me about father brother lover
      the word your word
    of images and inscribed lady bits, one movement to the next

you make this thumping sound
    bind us together show me my left arm all wrinkled name me woman
when I am deflated or too proud, it is what you believe you need as a man

tell me

      can you make me whole
    give me posture and bless me with the stubble
     of your voice beg for the paper bag chin tightness like pure
inflation if you are
      grinning nickel-eyed mouth nose sewn

maw

I am
not
a woman at
least
I think
so because
then
I would have
a tongue

tongue curled
in me holding
me
still

tongue that
cracks
thunder
tongue dumbbells
tongue beating me
back
to smile

I don't
have a tongue
I don't have
lips

I can't open
mouth
to draw
silver on ground
to spark each
row
of black thorn
spike leaf
shivering
through
the bush rush
of peach

no tongue no sea
on pinking green

no sense
of
delicacy

and if I were
to try
to be with a man
be for
him
a woman
I would want
so bad to
have him
kiss me

be
cause my not lips
keep clacking

white foam
over glass
and water his
whistle his
ffff to me
slip
spill
cartilage

my phone calls
all tongue
and teeth all
rambling and want
ribs bone
thick flesh
flaps on bumps on face
stumble
on roofs of mouths
the taste of me
so bitter
and thick

that we both
is broken
so I try to

teeth through
touch
not a
woman
not a cradle
not a soft
craft to sway

I am not
a woman
who can
hold the bruise
black forehead
pinched
him on my lap
his arms
reaching for my waist I
want his
body
enfolding
me my posterior
fit right not this
yapping
this
wasted
platitude

wake

I still   name things.   I still search
trick for kin   for kindness   on each elbow
my   bare knees.   I still wait for
morning the   showing
promising   clean   the sun to burn bed
good. I still   chew and swallow   feel each spoonful
go down   as if I were not there.
I still see   captions aching through me
the body heavy my mind pure white
ink dripping   inside. Somewhere in the spine or the marrow.
Semen   congeal   fat on the blade.

collateral contacts: a life

* me Mommy
* Johnson Elementary School
* Mommy
* Mommy Granny
* Edger Jr. High
* Mama
* Harrison Funeral Parlor Inc.
* Child Protective Services
* Children's and Family Services Division
* "Aunt" Barbara
* "Uncle" Eddie
* "Uncle" Eddie's hands
* Angel Heart Group Home
* Covenant House for Aged Out Foster Youth
* Him
* Him
* Him
* His mom's house
* Public Health Hospital
* Bus Station
* Marriage License Division, Hall of Justice
* David Earl with the van
* Public Health Hospital
* Diane Melborne from Social Services
* County Courthouse, Restraining Orders and Family Law
* Police Station
* Him
* Him
* Transitional Assistance Department

* Him
* Cash Advance Loan Company
* Motel on Palm and 8th Street
* Truck stop on 5th Street
* Corner of 14th and Grand Avenue
* Child Protective Services
* Booking Department, County Jail
* Him
* Sherita from Cell Block B
* Him
* Parole Officer
* Him
* Him
* Him me
* Department of Children's Services, Family Reunification
  Division
* Transitional Assistance Department
* Mama
* Granny
* "Uncle" Earl's hands
* me
* ~~Him~~ me
* Me

the boy at the gate

A little boy has
put his fingers
in the gate his

slender body
planted in stick
grass styrofoam

and potato chip
bag sprinkled
cool dirt. He is

all belly drooping
pants scabbed
knees. I know

he would smell of pee
and his face
would turn

like a leaf to the sun
of my touch.
But the drums behind him

ignorance
obscenities
monsters wild angry
cleaved

pull his
body from me
call him to
his knife of passage

shape him
into a naked

glistening thing
charred at each tip.

If only I could have got there first
swung him
over the gate to braid

his fingers in my limbs
hummed him laughter

dipped him in deep back
inside me until he
dissolves belly full of rice
bread or beans.

ag ora phobia

try drag.
and favor same.
sag
the now,
flag shame.
squir
t. ride rag.
mac, no,
mag
num.
numb nor
good god. brag.
game.
say me.
ap
pear human.
wag
in part,
each fleshy
cag
e.
say me
ss. act
or flayed sane.
mag
nificent no?
hagg
le a chor
us of more a

nd
just get
over
it.

blind

says join
in casualty   each spike
              cracks   don't
variations of   a   grin
    loot   little child

                           cracking
birth   us   the
clavicle
   killing him   how
        he try to   each
        groove   curbstreet
                        a suck
    snaking out   of space
    from the inside   It is

  why do we   against flat
     stay   one   irrigating
itself
               dimensional blades   in
     quiet   as if

  blind   and anyway
      him this prince
      a price

the little black girl

ask it. I know that smile. anything. how I hold up here, such hardness. how I cock sugar bags under my armpit. the baby. where I put my shoes. ask about the gray black the gunmetal. the powder or the knot, how it is tied what makes the cord so strong. or the girl. ask about the pacifier on ribboned string balled fist prints still on my skin. or better yet ask about the vial wobbling on that sharp precipice. scavengers as heroes. ask. question. give over to your rambling my own knees my doorsteps my breath. make drown a happy lightful thing. silence our sweet toy. if this before us is a pointed star then why choked sounds stiff and fuzzy. if instead it be a potted ring why not holla. when your mouth does that thing what theatre will it be that gathers around to feed. cows chewing grass or children a little black girl waiting for permission. who cries then coos then groans silent. are you anyway that baby. maybe she was big eyes. she will bake you a cookie this time brown and sticky and spread out over the pan or maybe this time my baby and I will finally talk my throat red rimmed straw fibers struck about it. the baby. the little girl. the baby the little girlthebaby thelittlegir

instinct

we'd watch
the butterflies sprout
from our fingers
drag our tails
through grass and mud
we'd hide inside
hollow foam
if only the music
would stop
playing our bodies beg
to grow still
the simplicity
of complex forms built
into a syntax
an infant
wiggling without shame
a spine curling
with pleasure but the music
keeps begging
us to stop concrete and fists
playing us
skinny blooms of
what we
pretend we should
be the beat downs the violins
overpowering the alto
parts of self
we could stop
use all four wings

the music keeps
 playing
 us hurting humaning
  us, booming
      between

scholarship

You did
not support
us. Rather we
exploded survived
even as your gravid
bodies swelled
and you gave over
to the slobbering
and you laughed and you ate.

You did not reach
down to pull
us up. You lay supine
reposed fat
legs splayed
with thick shins.
You eagerly
scratched each
shiny new root
ecstatic to wipe
the grease from
our lips our eyes.

No you did
nothing. We
appeared
spontaneously
a new breed
extended

stomachs curved
around our staffs
necks long
and thin the fingernail
adaptable
something bent
right, something
fitted
slashed into self
scrawled.

as by us.

As by other. These
people we call
peer. Your new.
Ideas of y'all. Flat
face. Caricature.
Fair use. Found
imagery. As be
experience. Research
the click
of tongue. Make
pring the holla. As
seem. As tend. Beat
down dance in
layer of line. Less
man than neck. Less arm
than ass. Fetch. Strike
dumb cuff
inhibition. Give
of your organ. Give up
flesh. Flail here
on shelf. Interact. Un
fold. Trust
us. Let us. Now
do it again. You
think we take
too much? Look. Look.
This brand new
thang. As
we paint. As you

step. Strum. As
we sell no
explore. As by
us. As is
ours. As if
still your. As
if still of.

very kind of hide

If you or me or us and them
Are bridges then what is it

The softness of my sister-friend the way
Of the ever omnipresent hide

An unscrubbed house clear face
Clean cheeks the wonder

On her wooly head
A whole world breaking like an egg,

Focusing always on the him
Walking toward her

What is this wetness

If not a sex or a callous
Act to hold a surface breech

My mama didn't have babies
My aunty never

Fought a day in her life
Anger a foreign thing in these palms

We black girls just wanting to be pink and dancers
But that wooden label

That arching gate stretches
Wide rubber masks over our

Wet, fur, settling, hide

consider this child adrift

a leg spools
a solitary foot out

to the lake
tapping slow

circles on the surface
daring

the unnecessary
a small purchase

in tender toefuls

that reflect and shift
the green down

to the coldness of
questioned measure

as if that stiff whim dared

to gather its body up
dive thick and proud a seed

tender
sliver a child's slow

learn to walk a mother

whispered warning like

weeds real as the water

cradling the tiny craft
the center

always spooling around her
because this space does

not send out its pliant lips

to pierce it just radiates
each touch

outwards desperate

where she is testing
a moment

lazy in its hum, possibility

its tiny pieces
each one bobbing

buoyant

the woven man

Taken very broadly these views are not mutually exclusive, since a woven man can be both cloth and wood. His form can be bought with the price of a look that lasts for four full seconds if one courts the quick peek and inability to unsee spoked feet. Taken to extremes the fabric of this man or the bark or the hood should be made into a pattern stole stiff by kneading the thread grain slow poured flesh to touch to trial to abstract idea then back to fiber and wood. Him peering through the sheer lace of you like a memory of an experience of a taste. Him watching as you wash the mud with pitcher and cup. Him as essential as the color of skin of this experiment (both internal and external) branching one straight arm into the filament or muscle of an exquisite sensation that is something close to pure pain or gratification or salt or cantaloupe or gravel or bruise. You must work until you are stiff until your joints are rippling ink and the quill droops or at least until the inability to make the effort of the shape to form consumes you. For this is cleave the molding of the body by hand to pinch and gloss and shape. Now my dear if you cheat and use knife or tool then the question of the woven man the question of these old scarves and wet leaves (black as peach pits) the stories of how it could be will wobble and fall roughly from bench and you will make yourself your own unjustified jail term or absent baby daddy or forfeited brother shape too soft to be plastic and too stark to be concrete. Remember your making is an issue not of your failing the choice given skin color hair face but of you learning proper technique.

ma'am

perhaps
it is
rubber
cloth   by each spike
thick   peeled raw
folded over flat heavy
with the burden   of use
bonded to the long dangling string

on the wall

in this disassembling business
razors teeth Pandaemonium
padlocked lips thick as marrow

he has her sit her twitch
muscles bleached creamed still he sits her
flicks her box gently so that

it trembles almost falls
but she stays in her perch
an egg Eve's mammy might have sucked clean
or else thrown down to grind like grain on ground

the girl tweaking : a story in units

chapter one—meeting a man in college and falling in love with it all

he wax blatant into probably. intertwining Asian, cock strut, tree.
two points for school prejudice, and truth. this ain't fish. if time
be an appeal, then I be an idealogy. so what the expressed hand?
they and we all speaking of single teachers. lord, this negativity.
the attitude may not be correct for communication. his accent
spends heads. them theyselves standard rules. his blatantness
hands us a probably, unfeathered and dressed. what could be up
next? shake off native, Dominican and Appalachian. yes it may.
that old world is all viewpoint and cue.

chapter two—in which our girl feels disappointed

carnival it. you cook and I pick. the knuckles tack sound heavy
on this here dust bridge. dirt drifts to lemme in. we release. the
sloppy kiss, a colony of leaves. is this red bliss? poison sometime
taste like syrup. such a thrill to be slipped in blizzard heat. his
hand placed just so on the machinery of knee. the murder of itch
is gold. you kiss carnival and make spectacle immaculate. are we
pasted bellies? however, no follow up. yes, baby do me pottery.
snake the finger in the closed slit. only provided we have enough
anti-freeze. shimmy shimmy shake, that upside down smile.

chapter III—that moment when she starts thinking about packing bags

when I answer the bell, I tend to drip. you faced every care in order to whine. brightest done that, by keeping the extension. this is woman fluid. amen. try not to ride our swans. oh now we didn't never name nothing waiting for a grey glass cakes. why you got to slow bleed? where is the attempt at least, the clean room? it is so hard to remember. just point and click, girl. every single bell, a small dawn playing each hair on an exposed brain. I didn't appreciate that. the shed of make might just be here. is this voice a part of my skin? keep on and keep on preaching.

chapter IV—our girl don't feel so good

the faults of each hour foresee blindness as an unaltered road. pressure is an old small night, possessed. I see tremble, then touch, then snow. he went and blotted out the slag, like some kind of Centaur. do mouths mast the sails in their heavy residue? we drew draft after draft. in the beginning there was an undertaking. grey-green eyes keep causing undue havoc. imaginary men scattered across the board. once, the when the breakage navigated the counter, we touched. I've never leaned on proof. each new page and new hour of something wrong, unseen.

chapter V—yeah, yeah, yeah, making do

each vertebrae is so right in its little row. I offer you things that snap easily. don't resist or pick your teeth. and all the while we devouring the unkind. after the sampling, the noose. this is all true. he will eventually say the weekly baths were actually done in small puddles of mud. my first time eating steel.   rest little lion, on my shoulder and eat peach. our own crib awaits. all that honey seeping out the ear. the rope, the neck, the spine, all these, homemade.

chapter VI—in which our story ends

stay be dead combined by dead. this is an application to paint cats, or lynch tenants toasted in threes. soul situated and I keep losing it. why we always light settlements? sneak it in. punk. choose the survivor, the broken one, then climb on her pole. shall I jig the bracket and the wine? us almost animating time, fully bursting on more than nicotine. rugged men don't have time to garden. mockery is mirror truth. stay be dead and me sneaking into the melting machines of heaven. panic, kid, you innocent. searching for water do be like raising hell. everything will be okay. my point, sweetness, exactly.

* A unit is poem structure reminiscent of a jazz structure, created by Makalani Bandele, that consists of 16 sentences of different syntactic structures unconnected by implicit context, except for the first and twelfth lines which should relate.

preliminary versions

kind
of kinky
the next
draft. the mark. the coming
scratch.
something
heretical in the lay
of letter.
pencil all raised
and crossed.
ready. fat circles
clean
thin. a
hinge. wry.
a whipped slant.
skin in tapped vows.
rhymed whines. verbs
hymned. thighs spoken
length
set. a cock break
of each
word. as if win is ready
to wax and wed.
the next black
x. the shiny
wrinkled
curve. the scribbled
over. tomorrow. next
told. next tine. a debt

unquestioned,
a find send
in the deep,
of the hide. the next
now. the erase. rub.
down. it.
wait. ready.
wise.

toys

woman as exotic peak of fruit-woman as
juice-woman bitten-
woman running down the leg-woman
cored-woman profiled-
stretched-two women-planted-
woman on the block-woman and
man holding hands-woman talking to
the devil-woman as devil-woman
knocked-upside head-drag-woman to
and fro-woman fist-woman
maker-woman fitter-woman
frying dice-woman cocked-cowed
woman little boy woman-he she
said who-woman and god-in a row
boat-wet-weft-clipped-eagled-talking 'bout-
woman-cured-woman eyed-woman cut-cult-sew woman
up needle woman-pierce wig-thread-kink-woman
sexy stockinged-cold-
stacked-woman heel-sit-fetch-
go-forward woman-skinny jeans
curved-woman as curve-plump
woman-woman and children-milk
breasts-baby drink-gorge-woman-
dangling-flounced woman-moaned
little girl eased-dancing woman-woman
winged-made up woman-

woman inside woman–
circular sorted-woman blown up–than woman–
think-leak-shrink-woman women all–
woman-toyed–

thing was

it was candy
flames and
petals bags of
ungone you
sentry   a dance of
a machine   with wash through the room
touch embedded   and I wanted credit the feel of
pressure and presence   cream   linen
savior   feeling   that poured each   in my skin it was
for this   un   sermon   you and crowning
drooling   won   and found   clouded   the feeling
thirsty   a need   you   from neck   less
fool   to free   to knuckle   of the
thing was   how you   held
it was   moved
cream   like
that poured each   bather   cotton
merman   for this   in my sin it was
and found   drowning   you and crowding
you   cursing   me
reeling   cruelty
needing   thing was
kneeling   it was
to   me

53

quarantine as cure

nothing but
    my want of
   you a cheat
   dormant as a
threshold dragged
stiff

     knead me sordid
  until I hack
 your lift

    blue us with
   flagships 'til we be
    unfit

tictamony: a script

him axing   confligulation)there we born, in the middle of
more found, there we born, tailor zoot zipped, pianoland flayers,
there we up in the wring all dressed in doghouse suit, savior to
the cream, alligator toed, innocent(

her persory   *no talk, mind you, finer and change and dawn
and any I would use* no this sun, no wish pricks* like inside
a body don't want shoe trips cause then there be equal parts
lye( )I feel leased, part page, look same, save sun, end layer, wait
for color

him axing   )there we tipped on low brow like hot sauce
brass swimming in gumbo whistle train, mindng our wrist
lists—there we born and she come alone all satin potato skinned
pillowqueen, all did hair, lash lip, that she be(

her persory   there just this and anniversary* a change dawn
coming over me style and pushbean half plait
axing +cuff up—muttoning the hopscotch(
pursory he say cram like mineral, steel woman, he say single
border of more frown

       ————**him axing**   )and she say we stage her( )sell
her to hell, how here was pin song and blood—she sprayed out
on wood, flexed foot tapped—she say we cue her, overflowing
preach hands, jazzed in for the offering, pop jacks like bottle
beans, the owe up (-)
               +the old uh uh uh(
her persory   fame to seal in front with shithead mystery—he

say I be beauty under wasps toes, bull mouse to the every walk
cause I owed worse than then I old worse than them

him axing   =but don't you'd figure that whiff shit she jelly
would keep those thighs from snapping, or that trip nickel had
horns, man we all know squeeze milk is a slick voice and every
pearl want to stomp a trigger, specially like this(-----)

her persory   I owed* can you believe that* I owed flips, the
same as glad, moan grabs, the pluck I know ( ) I owed. I ain't
spot a soot stiff as that nor a crack brim whip and I tell that
to anyone

morning

You do not wake turning the cord of sunlight over each finger. The
light taps small holes between the sheets.

You should learn the pattern
of language the cadence, the swift speech. It feels truer than the
blanket
tight around your shoulders. The blanket
swaddling plastic arms. The arms
holding string. The strings
attached to your eyes. You could open your eyes. You could sing.
How the body aches for the scald of
sleep.

You lay out all your tools: scissors, pen, glue, story of green dragons,
hot comb, razor, cup of sugar, ziplock bag, baby boy, mask, and
smile.

Got to find yourself a you.
An apex that will draw you in lined up red pen marks, let you follow
like
a dog until you are full.

burden of teeth

The corners of the mouth are the most mobile part of the smile. Raise eyes and fix on a site distant like there a horizon, or a boiling view of the sea. Consider the trailing shore an image of hope. Curve each side upwards. Straighten head and back. The climax is nested in the influences read in each flash of teeth. Smile once, quickly. Then smile again and hold tight the heaviness of that pattern. Renewed strength can be found if the lips are turned down. Stretch the mouth, push out the tongue. Make sure to return to the original form very quickly. Rest sparingly to consider the case of upward mobility.

the man with the the

       so this blacktop backdraft border hump stole
you done gone and you done went and I would like a piece of
    it should hump fly the kite side the man with the the
           you done had and you should not cause I just did and so

you done gone and you don't when and I would like a pea of
        this be porn stole hideflapping all kinds of mighty
          you done had and you could not cause I justice and so
    this be whipwon more this be cartoon comedy

       this be beep on stole hideflapping all minds of kite ease
         we done put by we would not do I don't forget the
    this be whipwon more this be carts on homely
badass ass wind hot sooted slope patrol

        we done put wily would not do I done forget the
      how you cut kind tooth thing your baby grip sight
badass ass wind hot toothed slope patrol
    like the drop ring the conk think like a right by ride

      how you cut kind toothsinging baby grip sight
    so this blacktop backdraft border hump stole
   like the drop ring the conk thing like a right by ride
   it would hump fly the kite side the man with the the

push

      make   take

I can   the   I can   the

            white.   wings and hands

          shapes like   and crumble

oysters, them into

    shells

   raw dripping   crouching meat.

cocoons.   I can reach   a plate of meek

     into the birth   of my own measure   a split lip

        of will   inches   uncracked

      and give three   cracked

         make it feel   I can fold   it

           the nose   the idea   as if

              into   roll   pocket

I can suck   true stench   into my back

   the yoke   eye

    make it stick   and slip the liquid

   the thick globe of a face   have it watch

        inside it. I can arrange the limbs   grind it

      in full plastic runs   game it

             I can push, too

ampers ands: a love song

Just coming was a hiccup and   lazy sty I saw it and
Keep his voice like a ray of flimsy and   cropped cream and
begin on every more and   want him to teach and
Give me crippled better   and than bread and than step and
Exploding my gawk and   as if on memorize and
Corn fed and   I felt and   the sound of the lunge
him making earnest and
My black bone gaunt and   tell me how to globe this and
baby and   baby and
Tell me how to sift great and all war is pungent salutes and
Bewildered feening rubbery and fuzzy and   we now in love and
Say costume this big and   old gaudy pearls of poured sauce and
inject it your way and
Don't we got to lead game and   remember bits and
having consciousness subdued and
My bellowing subdued and   and my belly subdued and
strangled or high or whatever and
I think I bought my body and
Properly amazed and   for dazed and   four days and
for days and   fordays and and and and and and
and and and and and
and

the robot

flesh works
be it a center for control
or a needle
drawing hunger

Shelley makes a doll
and we all line up
to the disease
infatuation with our Haitian greys
black eyes naming us creature
heads swollen like
red grapes

build create sweating
rags of simularity
and dried blood
the stump a heartbeat
insistence of a night visit
or oil and the possibilities of Halperin's
metallic light

do sing Carpenter
of a seminal
fire complex
as a stretched
a figure dragging
delicate body slow
miserably needed build make
make me

for Lovecraft was right
                              everything needs
            to eat

speak, cling, spin: a quick bop

crackling a code, eating out
condition unwedding unboxing up
the riot and glass in the thick of meal
black as exhaust and a swagger,
inching along ten feet tall
a gassed now, persisting, begging to

climb on the back, and spin

or else splay an exchange
of the end, tip of the trigger, tongue
crimped grease and leaky ache
bagging a bellow, curling the shin
around straps, scratching urges
to eat the bare paths, and close
the noise points of humility

climb on the back, and spin

word to me brother, as if held, as if preached
to a hack end of heated street, tuned
to sweat rag, the insistence
born brushed breath of sashes
bound to waists, my body for you loud, clear eyed
noise stones of grasping needing loving shine

climb on the back,
and spi

boy at lake

                                        perhaps
        his shoulders
                        back expanding
                                        he
        like brown trout could have
                        mirror and clear   used torso
to see
        rocks soaping toe and thigh   to blue
he turns to   basin to brush
                he does not swim
        where I question

                                        breathe
move tail move gill   the cold honesty of
                                        wanting it
                edged tips
he stands his wings
                towards the beach
        why the borders   the dive
                the wall of mountains
                past the center
        why these palms pressed
on his silver skin

                                        always
        where is this calm
                        blessed   this
bedding   framed
                                        lake and want and boy

but mr. blue

Water tried
to hurt me. I
was fine with my people,
sweating in the

I was
in the dark down and I
saw the

I was following
some newness home loud
repeating sass
tongue full of

Water
all dry bank and

Water
like bark
turned and

Water like
winter over
said

Me quiet breathe soak
and sing storm like
ash ribbon but

Water
wet pinned to

Water
sat too close to

Me all
me pickled up
washing the bald
roads of my

And wasn't it
Just like scalp
and my pulse
kicking to
the rhythm
of every
spackled word.

Water.

I tried to

I poured my

Sirens gurgling
warnings it will hurt
drip

How that thirsty mouth of thrum
did

How I hungered for my soles to drizzle
back for my wrists to cradle
the

But water

That river and

A basin a shiny hole the horn
that

The bend and the blues
man under
 each

and suddenly, bones

underneath my feet bird
like sticks that crackled
under the press of each
heel down to the faces
of my own
little girls that shook
up dust and sweat and
skin as if
I were breathing
tiny needles slivers
silky pieces of chalk
and I don't want to feel this
clumsy don't want to
see these
scars snaking thin don't want
to watch as flat feet flee
this is a graveyard
and I am stepping on
bones and I know I
screamed because I did
not know if I could keep
standing
seeing myself down in that
dirt asleep
on half-formed
fantasies screaming
back at me it happened it is
happening he is trying to touch
that child

bones in hair
heels my teeth
these white
knives these
gristling memories
I looked
down
at bones and
all I could do
was fall to my knees

slumbers for girls

Think about the way you learned.
A thick pulpy drink.
Cold pieces of salt meat. Think
about the stash under the bed. Getting soaked. Probably.

You can prop
each one up on a stool. They get so damn excited.
A delicate story.
Sniff skin and hair as you need.

Let them see you frown. There is still the matter
of the toothbrush. Wipe each
mouth free of debris. Avert the look.
It will hurt you or make you think. Bring out for them lots of grease.

The clamor they make is so slight. Move, you think, dance, speak.
Touch their arms, then let them play.
Hide yourself in the braid of the trees. Were you really
twelve or fifteen? Were you ever that clean?

Flowers, they ask for, curved shoes, jewelry. Their hunger
opens closet doors. Do they even know
how to scream? At certain angles they
look like grandma's fingers. Grasping, touching, questioning.

You will have to unlock the front door.
Trust the giggling. Not your tendency to disappear and dream. No one
is coming here tonight. No pale men
no monsters no thieves.

heaven

I
am slowly allowed to patrol
            Gambler shoes. The scream
       only a saxophone. Saturdays
            in carved jazz. Country clusters
       of gold, the way they walk
in heels. Here a thang asleep in
                    perforated sheets, lizard legs
    peeking through the black handfuls
of maze. Them making talk making orgies
lip power and lead gold, boats
       in the body my sneak and listening to
              throes curled like glitter. Mermaids
    twerking on candied feet. And coin. There
       by the arch, a man farmed slick, his
    hair bunched bushes, cat eyes restored
    reservoir. Ministers not needed, for
       the sober syncs to soar.
          This winking
  sun caught smoke keeps tickling
              it all the dolls the feet. This whore
              of jump and grin. An angry 'stache of physic.
       A gorge of cool ice sweet coal. Heaven, like wet
  nightmare, like swirl storm, like rest. And
                        I don't dare crave sleep. One hour
                              is enough.

hummingbird

A numbing
made of many
wings. A kissing
so fast they look
like blurs. A plump passive
drop of fur
with all the swirl and anxiety
of a city's veins
hovering past its
puff head to create
an irritating song in this drain
like voice and humility.
An awareness of good;
a need to make to
control each cloud
of jewels, the child's
mispronunciation,
the cold in the back
corner, her own
foolish dreams. She keeps
a bubble
around herself
and it is
not bad the layers
because a wall can be made
of static vibration, not
not stopped, but settled
assumed where the paths
are walkable despite

the odd looks
of a black girl as stranger
or rebar to guard
the body against
the gunshot the frown-look
the need to press small
where it can to
gold the air,
dot each beat with
falsetto: feathers
dry winking wings
and her hope for love maybe
right there the frantic motion
propelling her
to keep murmuring
for more.

at the door

good peoples ladies and young
foolish boys skirted gentle
humans invite me in. this mantled porch
cracked with cupped wind, grains of time
is hard to these damp knees. these knees slick
with splintered blinking their
thin hatred at back at me. door

touching my palm like a fist or a kiss like a
village vision water still sun boil
warm. invite me to soup and brown
brown cleft in two passed about the young
girl washing down the table
stealing dram and seed from plate fingers
in pie pan roil with beatitude rim bliss

and my arms all shaky. I seen
a tree made of human hands shackled
clean to the age rings leaves cloaked in
an old boxer's russet throne. I seen
runnels of faces stalked by me
the turn of one ripple a seeking eye
threatening violence or brute

kindness or a what I don't know.
I got only the joints left the girlish
tendons so much stretched jerky. I sold
everything bag full of stars smelt in sugar
skin always such sugar my sugar to draw each

beast forth to a maybe nod. once I pulled up
a small child from the muck and she stabbed me

right here too busy gumming to mind
the scar. open this wall, you damn teenagers
ladies please young men have mercy
and part your gilded teal surf. shit. don't you
know this rude. I can see you fisted forked
fiend greasing I can smell it you know the frying
the burning spice the young wine the joint the sweet
meat. and good lord I need.

as if we could fill ourselves

we keep kiss
feeding each other our
               lime yellow cheeks all
                     a one
        and one in reverie wise broken
tendencies that cup
like myths
musicians implied with the obedience
           of puppeteers we drape
       my longest skirt on the table set
           vase and fork flinch
as the roughness of my elbow brushes
past your hair hunger and a hint
of shyness a singular weight
making me know you know you
know it too a pendulum
that pierces the mirror and means
          you are not my lover but
I think
of fickle shadows on the dry
ground a hardness that
upsets each stretched grain the pull
            of you to me
         when I let you be
     the salt rubbing the brown
       webs the pinch of gold
         from my mouth full
water they made you calm
silent under my cheek where

I didn't know father his name

                              absence

                  chalk and honey

            waving making
me a sprawled gift that grew
me small
and smaller even as I learned to
                        cough out tiny fish
bones flesh enough to fill in
the holes it was the same
wound for you I think your mother
                  weeping slow her lose
of picture of you all this time
                  this plain pan rubbing out
family unrolling us from each
you would think me too hard
I would ignore your need
I understand
                  it now finally the rolled red
                  stuff of shoulders stiff as cold
dough pinched and edged
with salt to lay us
      flat on the roof of the mouth us
                  listening to our shadows
and memories us us again a necessity
chewed morsels
                  hard then pulpy then bit up
                              then

Acknowledgments

what is home *(words)*   Apercus Quarterly, 2012

consider the child adrift   ladies, please (Chapbook),
Dancing Girls Press, 2013

collateral contacts   The Newer York, 2013

tell me grinning man   Apercus Quarterly, 2012

the robot *(flesh works)*   Blackberry Magazine, 2013

slumbers for girls   ladies, please (Chapbook),
Dancing Girls Press, 2013

the doll on the wall   Sand Canyon Review, 2014

preliminary versions   Vinyl, 2016

as by us   Black Earth, 2016

the woven man   Kelsey Street, 2017

the little black girl   Kelsey Street, 2017

hummingbird   Motion Poems, (forthcoming) 2017

wake   Hilal If You Hear Me (2018)

Nikia Chaney is the author of two chapbooks, *Sis Fuss* (2012, Orange Monkey Publishing) and *ladies, please* (2012, Dancing Girl Press). She is founding editor of shufpoetry, an online journal for experimental poetry, and founding editor of Jamii Publishing, a publishing imprint dedicated to fostering community among poets and writers. Highly active in her community, Nikia has won fellowships and grants from Cave Canem, the Millay Colony for the Arts, Squaw Valley, and the Barbara Demings Fund. Nikia's poetry has been chosen by Nikki Giovanni as the winner of the 2012 OSA Enizagam Poetry Award. Of her poem "the fish," Ms. Giovanni writes, "…What power this poem has with showing the difficulty of growing up with a terrible secret. What a powerful song this friend sings for a friend drowning in if not evil, then certainly, difficulty." Her poem, "hummingbird" was used as inspiration for an original score and a forthcoming video by Motionpoems. As the fourth Inlandia Literary Laureate for the Inlandia Literary Arts Institute (2016–2018), Nikia hopes to help highlight the voices of San Bernardino, "this city that sits below mountains and deserts," its history, the people, the community, and what people really know of it through her poetry and by hosting workshops that address and heal violence.

by Tyler Atwood
an electric sheep jumps to greener pasture

by John W Barrios
Here Comes the New Joy

by Eirean Bradley
the I in team
the little BIG book of go kill yourself

by Suzanne Burns
Boys

by Calvero
someday i'm going to marry Katy Perry
i want love so great it makes Nicholas Sparks cream in his pants

by Leah Noble Davidson
Poetic Scientifica
DOOR

by Rory Douglas
The Most Fun You'll Have at a Cage Fight

by A.M. O'Malley
Expecting Something Else

by Stephen M. Park
High & Dry
The Grass Is Greener

by Christine Rice
Swarm Theory

by Michael N. Thompson
A Murder of Crows

by Sarah Xerta
Nothing to Do with Me

edited by Cam Awkward-Rich & Sam Sax
The Dead Animal Handbook: An Anthology of Contemporary Poetry

CPSIA information can be obtained
at www.ICGtesting.com
Printed in the USA
FSOW03n0017230218
44612FS